The Story of Our Holidays

EARTH DAY

Joanna Ponto

Enslow Publishing
101 W. 23rd Street
Suite 240
New York, NY 10011
USA

enslow.com

Published in 2016 by Enslow Publishing, LLC.
101 W. 23rd Street, Suite 240, New York, NY 10011

Library of Congress Cataloging-in-Publication Data

Ponto, Joanna.
  Earth Day / Joanna Ponto.
    pages cm. — (The story of our holidays)
  Includes bibliographical references and index.
  Summary: "Describes the history and traditions of Earth Day, including a craft and recipe"—
Provided by publisher.
  ISBN 978-0-7660-7457-6 (library bound)
  ISBN 978-0-7660-7469-9 (pbk)
  ISBN 978-0-7660-7463-7 (6pk)
  1. Earth Day—Juvenile literature. 2. Environmentalism—Juvenile literature. 3. Environmental protection—Juvenile literature. I. Title.
  GE195.5.P67 2015
  394.262—dc23
                    2015031043

Printed in the United States of America

To Our Readers: We have done our best to make sure all website addresses in this book were active and appropriate when we went to press. However, the author and the publisher have no control over and assume no liability for the material available on those websites or on any websites they may link to. Any comments or suggestions can be sent by e-mail to customerservice@enslow.com.

Portions of this book originally appeared in the book *Earth Day: Keeping Our Planet Clean*.

Photos Credits: Cover, p. 1 Ruslan Guzov/Shutterstock.com; p. 4 NASA; p. 7 TTstudio/Shutterstock.com; p. 10 Robert W. Kelley/The LIFE Picture Collection/Getty Images; p. 11 Santi Visalli/Archive Photos/Getty Images; p. 14 John Storey/The LIFE Images Collection/Getty Images; p. 17 © AP Images; p. 20 Matt Smith/Express-Times/Landov; p. 22 Timmary/Shutterstock.com; p. 24 ERproductions Ltd/Blend Images/Thinkstock; p. 26 Monkey Business Images/Shutterstock.com; pp. 28, 29 Karen Huang.

Contents

Our planet is a pretty special place! We need to keep it clean and healthy.

Chapter 1

Our Green Planet

The planet known as Earth is our home. It is the only planet that has people living on it. It is also the only planet with animals, trees, and flowers. That makes it a special place.

The Perfect Planet

What if Earth were a perfect place? What if Earth were a place that was always clean and green? There would be fresh air everywhere. Clean water would flow in our rivers. Everyone would have a garden or at least live near a park.

Trees would line our streets. They would shade our homes and schools. There would be large open areas, too. People would live close to trees, mountains, oceans, and living things.

The Real Thing

Sadly, Earth is not that way. There is a reason for that. We are not taking care of the environment—our natural surroundings.

Our Unique Earth

Earth is the third planet in the solar system. The other planets in our solar system are very different. Some planets are covered with atmospheres of poisonous gas. Other planets have little atmosphere at all. Earth is the only planet that has people living on it.

Factories and cars release dangerous fumes—smoke or gases—into the air. In some cities, the air is not safe for people to breathe. Garbage is being dumped into our water. This kills fish and other living things. It also makes many places unsafe for swimming. Garbage dumps across America are overflowing. Cities, businesses, and people create tons of trash.

Such damage to Earth is known as pollution. But it does not just happen in cities. Farmers sometimes put chemicals called pesticides on their crops. The pesticides kill bugs that harm crops. But they also kill wildlife and are dangerous for people to breathe.

Forests are disappearing. They are being cut down for wood or to make room to build. Often, forest animals lose their homes. Earth has become less green. It has also become less clean and less beautiful.

Making Changes

Some people are trying to change that. There is a special day to honor and protect our planet. It is known as Earth Day.

Earth Day is held every year on April 22. It is a day to think about the environment. There are meetings, fairs, and rallies. People plan ways to make things better. They clean up lakes and rivers. Trees and gardens are planted. Many people of all ages take part. That is because Earth belongs to all of us. We are all responsible for it.

Factories cause some air pollution. Their dangerous smoke and gases are not safe to breathe.

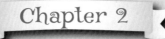

Chapter 2

Earth Day History

Earth Day is a new holiday. We did not always need a special day for Earth. The American Indians were the first people here. They took care of the land and used it wisely.

Progress . . . and Pollution

In the 1600s, people from Europe arrived. Things began to change. In time, fields gave way to farms, towns, and cities. Businesses opened and factories were built.

The population grew, too. More people needed more things. So businesses produced more goods. Cars and buses replaced wagons pulled by horses. There were superhighways instead of dirt roads. These changes are known as progress. Progress is supposed to be a good thing. In many ways, it is. But it is not always good for the air, land, and water.

Yet, few people thought about this. Earth's gifts seemed endless. But we learned that they were not. By the early 1960s, our air, land, and water were badly polluted.

Time to Clean Up!

Gaylord Nelson was governor of the state of Wisconsin. He saw the problem, and he wanted to change things. So he went on a speaking tour across America. He visited more than twenty-five states. He asked people to try to clean up the environment.

Nelson thought that having an Earth Day would be a good start. He knew that college students sometimes shared ideas in a special way. They held teach-ins. At these meetings, the students talked about problems. They worked on ways to change things. Nelson

American Indians

The American Indians took good care of the land. They were smart about how they used it. They did not pollute the land or the streams. They did not waste food, water, or trees. American Indians did not think that the land belonged to the people. They said that the people belonged to Earth.

Governor Gaylord Nelson asked people to help clean up Earth.

wanted to hold a huge teach-in for Earth Day.

Gaylord Nelson knew he could not plan Earth Day alone. He asked a college student to help him. That student's name was Dennis Hayes. Like Nelson, Hayes cared about the environment. A special office was set up in Washington, DC, to plan Earth Day. Other people came there to help.

Earth Day's Birthday

The first Earth Day was held on April 22, 1970. Twenty million Americans took part. They were from towns and cities all over the United States. More than two thousand colleges throughout the United States held Earth Day events.

In New York City, several streets were closed to cars. The space was used for an Earth Day fair. Students in Omaha, Nebraska, wore gas masks that day. They wanted to make people more aware of air pollution.

In Florida, people marched outside a power company. They brought along twenty pounds of dead fish. The power company had been releasing hot water into the bay. This caused many fish to die. The Earth Day marchers hoped to stop this.

A goat took part in Earth Day in Centralia, Washington. The goat was put out on a lawn. It had a sign on it that said, "I eat garbage— what do you do for the environment?"

An Earth Day fair was held on April 20, 1970, in New York City. Streets were even closed for the fair.

The first Earth Day was a huge success, and there were many neighborhood cleanups. People picked trash and litter out of rivers. They planted community gardens in empty lots. Thousands of Americans promised to make Earth a cleaner planet.

Taking Care of Our Earth

Earth Day changed the way we look at our environment. It made people more aware of problems. Earth Day also made government officials more aware of the need for changes.

Soon, some valuable changes occurred. The Environmental Protection Agency was established. It is a government agency that helps keep the environment safe. The Clean Air Act and Clean Water Acts were also passed. These laws protect the environment, too. The Endangered Species Act was passed, as well. This law protects animals. Many animals had become extinct, or died out. They had been killed by hunters or died when their homes were destroyed. Other animals were close to dying out.

Earth Day 1970 became an important day in our nation's history. It was the birth of the modern environmental movement. This united Americans in protecting the planet.

Chapter 3

Earth Day Today

Earth Day did not immediately become the annual holiday it is today. In fact, the next Earth Day after the first celebration in 1970 was twenty years later in 1990.

Saving the Planet

People had not forgotten that special day. Many still hoped to save the planet. They formed groups to protect the environment. Some groups worked on stopping pollution. Others worked to save wildlife. Still others tried to protect the forests.

Over time, they each had some success. However, these environmental groups felt we needed another Earth Day. Some

13

group leaders met with Dennis Hayes. They wanted him to plan an Earth Day for 1990.

Hayes was no longer a student. Now he was a lawyer. But he still wanted to help. He left his job for a while. He needed time to work on this project.

Dennis Hayes quit his job to plan a 1990 Earth Day celebration.

A Global Celebration

Hayes's work paid off. Earth Day 1990 was a worldwide event. Two hundred million people in 141 countries took part. This was important. No one country can protect Earth by itself. People from around the globe have to help. Different countries need to work together.

On Earth Day 1990, millions of trees were planted in South America. In Japan, there were meetings about pollution. Canadians declared war on litter. Small armies of people took part in cleanups.

Groups in the United States were especially busy. There were both land and river cleanups. Acres of trees were planted. Many towns held Earth Day fairs. People at these events served delicious organic foods. These are foods grown without the use of pesticides.

After 1990, things changed. Earth Day was held every year. This has been good for the environment. People need to remember our planet. Earth deserves its own day.

Gaylord Nelson continued to help. He became known as the Father of Earth Day. In 1995, Nelson was awarded the Presidential Medal of Freedom. This is one of our nation's highest honors.

Earth Day 2000

Every Earth Day has been important. But Earth Day 2000 was extra special. That was Earth Day's thirtieth birthday. It was also the first Earth Day of the twenty-first century. More than five hundred million people from many different countries took part.

The United Nations (UN) in New York City had an Earth Day celebration, too. The United Nations is a group of people from almost all of the world's free countries. The UN works for world peace. One child from every country in the United Nations took

Healing Our Planet

Our planet is sick because we have not taken good care of it. On Earth Day and every day, we work to make it better. Together, we can work to stop pollution. We can save wildlife. We can protect our forests.

part in the celebration. The children dressed in costumes from their homelands. Each planted an olive tree, a symbol of peace, in the UN's garden. During the ceremony, 189 white pigeons were set free. There are 189 countries in the UN.

Many Earth Day events were held in other parts of the United States. There was an Earth Day fair in Washington, DC. Movie stars and elected officials spoke to the crowd. They urged people to care for the environment. Thousands of people listened and applauded.

In Louisville, Kentucky, more than thirty thousand trees were planted. An Earth Day hike was held in Eugene, Oregon. The hikers enjoyed being in the wilderness. They also talked about ways to protect it.

Scuba divers were active, too. They had their own Earth Day 2000 event. It was called Dive into Earth Day! The divers cleaned up beaches. They also did underwater cleanups. More than twenty-five hundred divers helped. They picked up about thirty-five thousand pounds of trash.

Earth Day is not a national holiday. Each state decides for itself how to celebrate. Banks and businesses do not close. Mail is delivered that day. But it is still an important day. Earth Day is a reminder that we must respect and protect our surroundings.

Students in New Delhi, India, celebrate Earth Day, too. They gather together to bring attention to the Earth.

Chapter 4

An Earth Day School Day

On Earth Day, classrooms all over the world are filled with activity. Thousands of students from all over the United States take part in the Earth Day Groceries Project. Students draw pictures about Earth on large brown paper bags. Some people write Earth Day messages on the bags, too.

The bags are put in stores on Earth Day. When people buy something, it is put in one of the bags. This reminds people to think about the environment. It is also just one fun way to spread the word.

Recycling Projects

Students do other things, too. In one Tennessee school, each student brought in a nickel. The money was used to buy a tree that the students planted on Earth Day.

The Earth Day Groceries Project

Students from all over the United States create some fun Earth Day artwork. The Earth Day Groceries Project is on the Internet for everyone to see. For more information on this fun website, go to earthdaybags.org.

Many young people work on recycling projects. Through recycling, old items are reused, and then they are made into new things. This creates less waste.

For Earth Day, some students in Louisiana recycled newspapers. They collected the newspapers and took them to local recycling centers. The students saw that their work counted. Paper is made from trees. Recycling newspapers saves trees. Every nine grocery bags that the students filled with newspapers equaled one tree saved.

Other students recycled, too. They put on Earth Day fashion shows by wearing recycled fashions. Their outfits looked new, but they were made out of old clothes.

Recycling was part of some Earth Day art shows, too. Students made recycled sculptures. They used old toys and common household items to make Earth-smart art.

Students in Upper Mount Bethel, Pennsylvania, create games out of recycled materials.

Schools Saving Energy

In many schools, students find ways to save energy. This helps the environment. Oil and gas are used for energy. These things come from deep within our planet. But they will not last forever. We need to conserve or save oil and gas. Using less energy also keeps the air cleaner.

Some California students formed energy patrols. The patrols shut off the lights when classes leave the room. This saves energy during lunch and recess periods. The patrols also make Save Energy signs. They put these next to all the light switches. The idea is to tell others to use energy wisely.

T-Shirts and More

Schools do other things for Earth Day, as well. Sometimes they plant gardens. They can make a vegetable soup from the veggies they grew themselves! See page 22 for a great recipe to try.

Sometimes they put on Earth Day plays. They have Earth Day fairs and poster contests. At times, students dress for Earth Day. Their schools may ask them to wear a special T-shirt that makes people think about Earth Day. The shirt can have a picture of Earth on it, or it can show an endangered animal. Some shirts have Earth Day messages printed on them.

Earth's resources are limited, but the ways we can protect the planet are not. Many schools are proving this is true.

Earth Day Vegetable Soup*

Ingredients:

3 tablespoons (45 mL) olive oil

(1) 8-ounce (230 g) can of red kidney beans or chickpeas

(1) 8-ounce (230 g) can diced tomatoes

3 stalks of celery, diced

4 potatoes, diced

3 medium carrots, diced

1 onion, diced

3 cloves of garlic, minced

3 cups (720 mL) vegetable stock

¾ cup (110 g) shredded cabbage or kale

1 zucchini or yellow squash, sliced into 1/4-inch (6 mm) rounds

¾ cup (110 g) each of your choice: green beans, lima beans, corn, or any other vegetables you have on hand

1 tablespoon (15 mL) Worcestershire sauce

1 teaspoon (5 mL) paprika

1 teaspoon (5 mL) black pepper

½ teaspoon (2.5 mL) turmeric or curry

3 bay leaves

2 tablespoons (30 g) fresh thyme, pulled from the stem

Directions:

1. In a large soup pot, combine olive oil, potatoes, and carrots over medium-high heat. When carrots and potatoes start to brown slightly, add onions, celery, and garlic.

2. Add spices, herbs, Worcestershire sauce, and stock. Bring to a boil.

3. Add tomatoes, beans, and other vegetables. Cover and bring back up to a boil.

4. Turn heat down to low.

5. Let simmer at least 30 minutes (the longer it simmers, the more the flavors will blend).

6. Add cabbage or kale and cook 5 more minutes, or until the greens are wilted.

7. Serve with warm, crusty bread.

* Adult supervision required.

Chapter 5

Earth Day Every Day!

It's easy to take care of Earth every day! Try some of these Earth-saving tips:

- Take showers instead of baths. Showers use less water.

- When brushing your teeth, do not let the water run. This wastes a great deal of water.

- Shut all faucets tightly. Leaky faucets waste water.

- When leaving a room, remember to turn off the lights, television, and computer. This saves electricity.

- Avoid single-serving containers. The packages they come in create extra unneeded garbage. Some toys have too much packaging, as well. This is done to make the toy

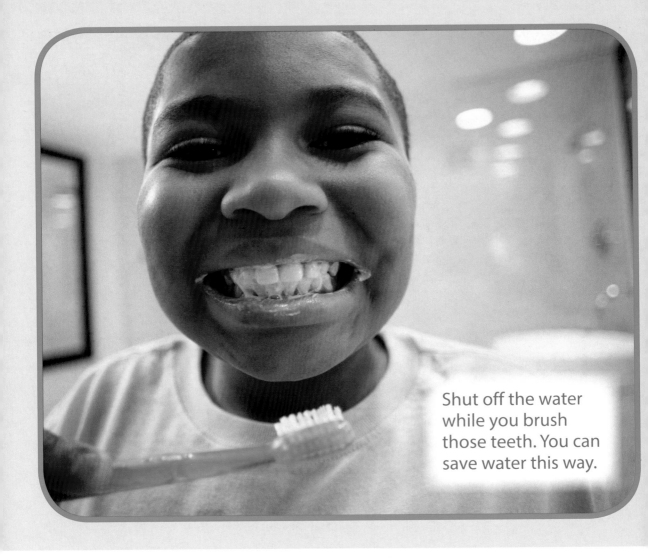

Shut off the water while you brush those teeth. You can save water this way.

look better. It is not better for the planet, however. It does not make the toy any more fun to play with, either. Think of the environment when you shop. Buy Earth-smart things that do not come in too much packaging.

- Recycle what you have outgrown. Many charities accept old clothing. Hospitals and daycare centers take old toys. Libraries often accept used books. They sell them at book sales. That means more money for new books. It also means less garbage.

- Do you bring your lunch to school? Try carrying it in a reusable bag. Paper bags increase waste. Try to reuse grocery bags from stores, or take a cloth tote bag with you instead. It can be used again and again. If you have paper and plastic bags, see if you can find ways to use them again. How many uses can you get out of one bag?

- Do not always ask for a ride. Cars cause air pollution. Bicycles do not. They do not give off fumes. Neither do your feet. Think twice when you are going somewhere. Can riding a bike or

Plastic and Pollution

Petroleum-based plastic products now take up about 25 percent of the volume of landfills. Instead of using petroleum-based plastics, we can use plastic bags and wraps made from an Earth-friendly starch-polyester material.

If you bring your lunch to school, use a lunchbox or other bag. You can use it over and over again.

walking get you there? Those would be better choices for the environment.

- Write, write, write. Let other people know how you feel about the environment. Put your thoughts in a letter. Try writing to your local newspaper. Your letter might be printed or posted on the Internet. Write to elected officials, too. Your parents or a librarian can help you find the addresses.

These are just a few of the things you can do to help the planet. Can you think of others? If so, try them. Earth is the only home we have. We need to take care of it on Earth Day and every day.

Earth Day Craft

It's easy to make a simple but creative Earth Day gift. If you wrap these stone paperweights as gifts, try to use recycled paper. The stones also make great room decorations. They are fun to collect and trade, too.

Here are the supplies you will need:

a smooth stone (any shape)
a colored pencil
a paintbrush
poster paints

Directions:

1. Wash the stone well. Let it dry for at least one day.
2. Use the colored pencil to draw something on the stone. You can create a nature scene or an animal. You might prefer to just make a design. You can erase any mistakes if you use a pencil.
3. With the paintbrush and the poster paints, paint over what you have drawn.
4. Let the stone dry overnight.

Make an Earth Day Paperweight

*Safety Note: Be sure to ask for
help from an adult, if needed,
to complete this project.

Glossary

conserve—To protect or use carefully.

endangered—At risk of dying out and disappearing completely.

environment—Our natural surroundings.

extinct—An animal or plant that no longer exists.

natural resources—Anything of value found in nature, such as water, soil, forests, and wildlife.

organic foods—Foods grown without the use of chemicals.

pesticides—Chemicals that kill insects in crops.

pollution—Damage to Earth's land, air, or water.

Presidential Medal of Freedom—The highest honor that can be awarded to someone who is not in the United States military.

recycle—To reuse something.

Learn More

Books

Appleby, Alex. *Happy Earth Day!* (Happy Holidays!) New York: Gareth Stevens, 2013.

Green, Robert. *From Waste to Energy* (21st Century Skills Library: Power Up!). Ann Arbor, MI: Cherry Lake Pub., 2013. Kindle ed.

Hayes, Amy. *Celebrate Earth Day* (Our Holidays). New York: Cavendish Square Publishing, 2014.

Paul, Miranda, and Elizabeth Zunon. *One Plastic Bag: Isatou Ceesay and the Recycling Women of the Gambia.* Minneapolis, MN: Millbrook Press, 2015.

Websites

Earth Day Bags
earthdaybags.org
Learn all about the Earth Day Groceries Project, get your own project started, and see what other kids have made.

Earth's Kids
earthskids.com/earthday.htm
Learn about Earth Day and how to start your own celebration.

Learning and Teaching about the Environment
epa.gov/students
At this website, kids of all ages can research information and project ideas for saving the environment.

Index